Mahrokh Daneshnia

# An Analysis of the Interaction between the Editing/Montage and Spectator

GRIN Verlag

**Bibliografische Information der Deutschen Nationalbibliothek:**

Die Deutsche Bibliothek verzeichnet diese Publikation in der Deutschen National-
bibliografie; detaillierte bibliografische Daten sind im Internet über http://dnb.d-
nb.de/ abrufbar.

**Imprint:**

Copyright © 2013 GRIN Verlag GmbH
Druck und Bindung: Books on Demand GmbH, Norderstedt Germany
ISBN: 978-3-656-63724-0

**This book at GRIN:**

http://www.grin.com/en/e-book/271504/an-analysis-of-the-interaction-between-
the-editing-montage-and-spectator

**GRIN - Your knowledge has value**

Der GRIN Verlag publiziert seit 1998 wissenschaftliche Arbeiten von Studenten, Hochschullehrern und anderen Akademikern als eBook und gedrucktes Buch. Die Verlagswebsite www.grin.com ist die ideale Plattform zur Veröffentlichung von Hausarbeiten, Abschlussarbeiten, wissenschaftlichen Aufsätzen, Dissertationen und Fachbüchern.

**Visit us on the internet:**

http://www.grin.com/

http://www.facebook.com/grincom

http://www.twitter.com/grin_com

Mahrokh Daneshnia

Theory for Film Practice

February 22, 2013

An Analysis of the Interaction between the Editing/Montage and Spectator

This essay analyses early theories in regards to editing and montage as a film form and its relationship to the meaning that it creates in spectator's mind. The main statement to prove in this essay is that controlling editing methods ignores the spectator's imagination and conflictive editing is the right method to interact with spectator's mind creatively. The essay considers Hugo Munsterberg, Sergei Eisenstein and Vsevolod Pudovkin's essays by clarifying the major points and debating the similarities and dissimilarities between the three arguments.

The first essay to analyse is "The Photoplay" by Munsterberg. The German-American psychologist does not use the term "editing" in his work but he mentions parallel editing, cut backs, close ups, flash-forwards and flashbacks, which are his way of describing editing. He believes that the combination of different scenes, actions and rhythms and also enlargement of small details or close-ups, are all derived from the psychological process of the human mind. For instance when he talks about cut-backs or going back to an earlier scene, he considers the psychological aim of cut-backs the most interesting of all. Cutting back to a precedent scene recognizes the mental act of remembering and it forms the reality by the demands of our soul. The same principle stands true with flash-forwards, only this time they deal with the close or distant future and the mental process of imagination replaces the memory. The "photoplay" that is the word used by Munsterberg for film is capable of following the rules of mind rather than the restrictions of real world. Another method which Munsterberg discusses is parallel editing. He believes that unlike theatre, film has the ability to take the spectator into different spaces, ignoring all the geographical and physical limitations. In other words the photoplay makes it possible to mentally and visually travel through various imaginative worlds. Munsterberg is also interested in spectator's attention as another mental element. He believes that in theatre spoken word is the main tool to direct the spectator's attention. In photoplay, movements, close-ups and editing techniques replace the use of words and pictures control spectator's attention. In his opinion music and other noises do not offer the same importance as pictures do. What spectator perceives is controlled by the events on the screen and a series of exciting emotional events control the involuntary attention, forcing the spectator to react to certain actions.

Vsevolod Pudovkin the Soviet filmmaker is particularly interested in editing and montage. He suggests separate pieces create a film. Shots from different angles build scenes, scenes build a sequence and sequences together make a film. He calls this process Editing and describes the editing process of scene, sequence and scenario as controlling methods of attention. In his theory he argues that each shot is a piece which is there to represent the main action taking place in the scene and each piece is shot to guide the attention to what is important for filmmaker. Pudovkin also mentions parallel editing when he talks about editing the sequence. Again he indicates that it is the scenarist's duty to direct and shift the attention of spectator from one scene to another in an obligatory guidance of thoughts. Another significant matter that Pudovkin argues is Relational Editing which uses a number of editing methods to have an impression on spectator and to create tension and emotion. The first method is Contrast which means putting together separate shots from different scenes to create a contrast effect, obliging the spectator to compare both situations. He also mentions Parallelism again, this time in more details and by that he means, editing two separate scenes in parallel to each other to develop a relationship between them in spectator's mind. Symbolism is another method that creates only a mental perception by using a symbolic act. There is also simultaneity method mostly used in American films to develop two related acts at the same time, aiming to create the maximum amount of tension and emotion and finally the Leit-motif or reiteration of theme that is a method of repetition of a theme to put more stress on a subject by scenarist to underline an issue. Pudovkin is also interested in the significance of close-up and its aim in a scene. In his view Close-up is there to point the spectator's attention to the significant details that are vital to understand the story and without them the appropriate scenario construction is impossible.

Pudovkin and Munsterberg both show an interest in analysing editing and montage psychologically, but each has a completely different perspective. For Munsterberg different methods in filmmaking are aesthetics of film and these methods are extracted from human psychological and mental processes such as memory and imagination. For Pudovkin different editing methods and montage are means to unveil the character's psychological commotion. He believes that the filmmaker has all the montage tools in his possession and uses them to control and direct the mind of spectator into what he believes to be the right direction.

Sergei Eisenstein, who is known to be one of the most influential Soviet filmmakers and film theorists, challenges Pudovkin's theory and opposes him openly in his essay about montage. For Eisenstein montage is the combination of a series of shots which are neutral in meaning separately, but when composed together the result is a meaningful, intellectual concept. He clarifies his argument by using Japanese hieroglyphs and symbols and comparing them to individual shots in film. Each hieroglyph represents an object in real world and by combining two hieroglyphs a meaning is formed. For example the dog and the mouth, two unrelated objects, each represent an object but when combined together the meaning of barking which cannot be represented in one hieroglyph, is understood. In other words, the composition of two representations forms a concept in spectator's mind. Eisenstein suggests that this is very similar to what happens in cinema and montage. The shots are neutral on their own and unable to suggest a meaningful context and juxtaposing them creates a concept. He continues his argument by criticising the existing analysis in old school filmmaking indicating that the shot is an element of montage and montage is the assembling of elements. Eisenstein believes that such analysis is completely wrong and the shot is not an element in montage but it is a montage cell. He explains that montage is conflict, it is a collision of two factors and like any other art, conflict is the necessary trait for cinematic art. In a simple example, he likens the shots and montage pieces to explosions in a car engine and describes that they have the power to progress the film forward the way these explosions move the car forward.

Munsterberg focuses on the psychological or mental processes of spectator's mind used in film viewing prioritising those over other creative considerations. Although his view regarding the element of attention in spectator's mind is close to Pudovkin, both suggesting that spectator's attention is controlled by pictures, Munsterberg yet believes that film is an art form. In Pudovkin's theory, there is no consideration for spectator's mental and creative abilities. Spectator is forced to watch and accept the filmmaker's guidelines so there is only one way of perceiving the narrative. In other words the filmmaker is given the authority to control the viewer's minds, and decisions are already made, leaving no room and opportunity for the creative minds to engage creatively. Eisenstein opposes Pudovkin directly, condemning him for defending the montage process as a "series" against what he believes to be a conflict to engage the spectator's mind and not a "brick by brick" gradual progress. Eisenstein theory is the most accurate in comparison with other two as he considers fully the spectator's creative interaction with film. Unlike Pudovkin he believes that spectator is not a passive element who is only there to being told how to perceive a meaning only in one single way. Eisenstein gives the spectator the opportunity to think and imagine creatively and to comprehend a different meaning by basing the montage on conflict.

Works Cited

Braudy, Leo and Marshal Cohen. *film Theory and Criticism*. New York: Oxford
    University Press, 2009.

Munsterberg, hugo. *The Photoplay a Psychological Study*. D.Appleton and company,
    n.d.